D0426447

A gift for

From

Laughter & Latté

JOYFUL INSPIRATION
FOR WOMEN

COUNTRYMAN®

A Division of Thomas Nelson Publishers
Since 1798

WOMEN OF FAITH
BOOK SELECTION

© 2006 Women of Faith, Inc. All rights reserved.

Published by J. Countryman, a division of Thomas Nelson, Inc, Nashville, Tennessee 37214.

Project manager—Terri Gibbs

No portion of this publication may be reproduced, stored in a retrieval system or transmitted in any form by any means— electronic, mechanical, photocopying, recording, or any other—except for brief quotations in printed reviews, without the prior written permission of the publisher.

All Scripture quotations, unless otherwise indicated, are taken from the New King James Version (NKJV®), copyright 1979, 1980, 1982, Thomas Nelson, Inc., Publishers. Used by permission.

Designed by Olika Design Studio, Cincinnati, Ohio, 45210
www.studiolika.com

ISBN: 1-4041-0332-5

www.thomasnelson.com
www.jcountryman.com
www.womenoffaith.com

Printed and bound in USA

Contents

Introduction

Family

Faith

Acknowledgements

Life is precious, and every day is a new opportunity.
I want to wring all the joy out of it that I possibly can.

—Thelma Wells

Laughter
& Latté

Friends

**Friends
are the sunshine
of life.**

The Sunshine of Life

A poet once described friends as "the sunshine of life." I myself have found that the day is certainly much brighter when I'm sharing it with my friends. Enjoying fellowship is one of life's sweetest blessings and joys. What would we do without people and the many shadings of companionship and camaraderie? We need friends in our lives, friends with whom we not only discuss "deep" issues and confide our secrets, fears, or sorrows, but with whom we can laugh, play, and even cry. The best times in life are made a thousand times better when shared with a dear friend.

Camaraderie is definitely a part of friendship, and camaraderie itself can often produce friendships, too. When we reach out to others, they reach out to us. It's a two-way street, a street practically lined with balloons and streamers in celebration of the unique bonds of friendship.

Friends are indeed the "sunshine of life."

—**Luci Swindoll**
You Bring the Confetti

Throwing a party,
even if it's just a cup
of coffee shared,
is good for the soul.

Vivé la Friendship!

Girlfriends bring out so much in us that no man ever could. They understand us, they cry with us, they shop with us . . . no man does that! We are sisters who speak the same language, like the same movies, have similar dreams and goals, and eat more than we should. Vivé la friendship! . . .

What determines friendship? Something intangible, that won't be defined. Something inside clicks. Something in our soul responds like a flower opening to the sun. We can't specify it ahead of time, but we know it when we feel it. Friendship is a mystery. The solving of the mystery is impossible. When you ask lifelong friends why they are friends, they can't explain it. "We just are." Then they smile.

—Nicole Johnson
Fresh-Brewed Life

LUCI SWINDOLL: How do you view your place in the working world, Mary? Is it a profession or a calling?

MARY GRAHAM: It's completely a calling. But knowing me, it would be a calling if I worked at a coffee shop. I think of all the people who need something to drink and I could give them the perfect thing . . . a word of cheer or something with their coffee that could help them. Life is a mission, and I'm on it!

*The greatest
beauty is
inner beauty.*

Kaylan Pickford

7

Friendship & Afternoon Tea

$\mathcal{M}$y friend Charlotte and I were enjoying a delightful afternoon at Lake Como in Northern Italy with Magda Olivero, internationally renowned opera star. Magda especially wanted us to see the famous Villa d'Este, built in 1550, that was situated beside the lake.

Hotel officials greeted Magda warmly when we walked in. They knew her well and escorted us to a table near the window overlooking the lake. The view was breathtaking.

We ordered tea and my mind left the scene: *This is unbelievable. How can this famous woman, with all she has to do, take time to leisurely show us Lake Como? Give up an afternoon? Treat us like royalty? What kind of woman is this?*

The people at the hotel obviously loved her; they treated her like the great lady she is.

It's no wonder. Magda Olivero had enjoyed a remarkable opera career in Europe. Her sensitive interpretations of various roles had made her famous worldwide. At the time, Charlotte and I had known her only a year; we had been working with the Dallas Opera Company when Magda made her American debut there in 1967. But that day we felt like two of the most important people in her life. We didn't realize until later, as we had opportunity to know her better, that Magda made everybody feel this way.

—Luci Swindoll
Notes to a Working Woman

Parties in Our Souls

A couple of years ago, my friend Denise gave me the book *Here and Now* by Henri Nouwen. He taught me why birthday parties are so significant: "Birthdays need to be celebrated. I think it is more important to celebrate a birthday than a successful exam, a promotion or a victory. Because to celebrate a birthday means to say to someone: 'Thank you for being you.' On a birthday we do not say: 'Thanks for what you did, or said, or accomplished.' No, we say: 'Thank you for being born and being among us.'"

This is the heartbeat of celebrating friendship. Rejoicing, honoring, applauding, commending, saluting, toasting the wonderful people in our lives. Not for what they do, but for who they are, and for what they mean to us. "Thank you for being you." Throwing parties over friendship. Not just once a year on a birthday, but as often as we can. Parties in our souls. Gratitude. Celebrating life.

—Nicole Johnson
Fresh-Brewed Life

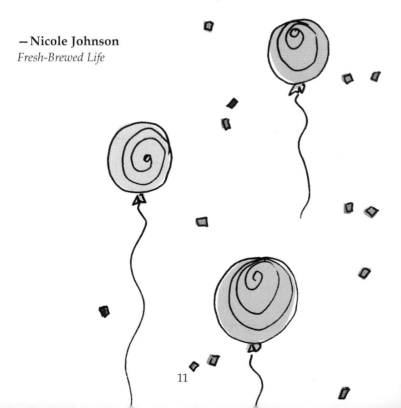

11

True friendships
are characterized by grace,
truth, forgiveness, unselfishness,
boundaries, care,
and love in gigantic
and mutual proportion.

Luci Swindoll

Celebrate!

Laughing with friends is just like eating cake at a party. You can have a party without cake, but who would want to? Every friend I have in my life knows how to belly laugh, and not take themselves, or me, too seriously. Laughter is like a tall, creamy, four-layered, beautiful cake that leans to one side. A cake that is meant to be cut and shared. Two forks and enjoyment beyond belief. . . . Celebration indeed!

— Nicole Johnson
Fresh-Brewed Life

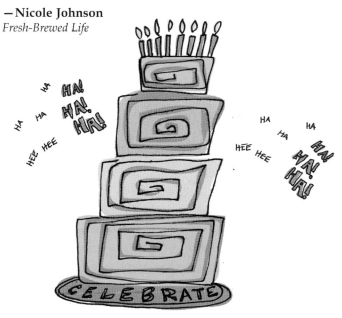

Friendship words:

Faithful

Funny

Fantastic

Forgiving

Fair

Flexible

Fabulous

First-rate

My Best Friend, Terry

$\mathcal{I}$ received my undergraduate degree from one of the strictest universities in the country. We could not hold hands with the opposite sex on campus. Our hemlines had to be a certain length. . . . We sometimes joked that one of us might be the first student shipped home because the dean of women found a hole in the *knee* of our bathing suit.

I didn't mind the rules too much, but my best friend, Terry, struggled with them. Only two weeks after we arrived she was caught holding hands with her boyfriend. She was sent a slip of paper indicating she had an appointment with the dean of women. Only a very serious offense would necessitate a meeting with the dean. I was nervous for my friend.

Terry entered the dean's office and was asked to sit down across from her at the desk. It was a long, impressive desk, with the wooden finish polished so perfectly you could see your reflection. The dean looked at Terry with penetrating steely gray eyes and spoke in a slow, Southern drawl: "My dear girl, what are you *saving* for marriage?"

Terry was so surprised by the question she felt like responding enthusiastically, "Why I'm saving *the other hand*, ma'am." . . .

Looking back on those four brief years of my life, I smile. Rules. Regulations.

Regimented skirt lengths. Chaperoned dating. Room inspections. Mandatory chapel. None of it seemed pleasant or desirable, but it did challenge me to form opinions about what's right and wrong, good and bad, essential and nonessential. . . .

And by the way, I've been married for a *long* time, and I *still* get a big thrill out of holding hands!

—Carol Kent
Detours, Tow Trucks, and Angels in Disguise

Friendship and Laughter

Laughter works on the soul like medicine. There are a couple of friends that I love going to lunch with. So much healing comes from laughter. We laugh about men, we laugh about longing for heaven. When we finally get around to looking at a menu, we laugh about our longing to be filled. When the waiter comes to take our order, we can hardly get the words out, as one of us invariably orders, "One of everything, please, with cheese." Our longings, as they are discussed with friends, create a bond that wouldn't come if we simply stayed on the surface. Real laughter and enjoyment come from going deep and then rising to the surface to get air. The laughter is like bubbles on the way up.

—Nicole Johnson
Fresh-Brewed Life

Fun

You look
FABULOUS
when you
laugh!

I Want My Old Neck Back!

$\mathcal{N}$ext time you see me, you may not recognize me. Just the other day I bought some wrinkle cream at Kroger that will start showing "visible signs of improvement in just fourteen days." I'm on day three. The product promises continued improvement, so by the time you and I happen to run into each other, I may look like I'm in my twenties. The label says a few drops will improve the appearance of my fine lines, but my problem is that I have a few lines that aren't so fine. In fact, a year or so ago, I looked in the mirror and I had on somebody else's neck. I don't know who she is, but I didn't ask for her neck.

I want my old neck back. So I'm using more cream than the label says. . . .

No, I'm not crazy about the physical effects of aging . . . but I am happier and more comfortable in my own (looser) skin than I've ever been. Not only that, like many of you, I live under unbelievable pressure, but actually, I am calmer and more peaceful than I've ever been.

The time-release on my ginseng must have just kicked in because now I suddenly remember one of those nine hundred and ninety-eight reasons why growing old is better. Sometimes we've allowed God to use the time to teach us a little more sense.

— Beth Moore
Feathers from My Nest

Joy is the one contagious disease that's welcomed by the medical community.

Do Your Best,
Laugh About the Rest

$\mathcal{M}$y philosophy is that we should just do our best—
and laugh about the rest. We have to keep things in
perspective. Sure we may be fat, ugly, and have the
fashion sense of Phyllis Diller, but as long as our
sense of humor is visible, we'll manage the rest!

Anyway, how did those single-digit sizes become
all the rage? Beauty seemed a lot more realistic—and
attainable—when terms like *voluptuous* and *ample*
were more common than the dreaded words *lean*
and *firm*. For many of us, it's quite comforting to
remember that Marilyn Monroe wore a size 12 and
that even though there are a handful of supermodels
who wear a size 8, there are three billion women
on the planet who don't!

—**Barbara Johnson**
Leaking Laffs

23

Get a Grip!

During a Women of Faith conference in Denver recently, a tiny mouse got on the porch where the speakers sit. Who knows how it got there? Perhaps it was fond of worship music and wanted to enjoy our singing up close and personal. I wish you could have seen the reaction of my porch pals when that little mouse showed up. Thelma shrieked, stuck her legs straight out in front of her and hid behind her purple purse the size of Kansas; Patsy sat on both legs until they disappeared: Sheila screamed bloody murder but didn't have to levitate since she spends her life on four-inch heels anyway; and Marilyn looked at the thing, and turned to me with, "I'll bet that mouse is scared to death of all these women."

I chided the whole bunch with a characteristically loving comment: "Roaches in Africa are bigger than this little varmint. Get a grip!" And we all went right back to singing "All Things Are Possible." (Fortunately, none of the eighteen thousand women in the audience knew what was happening or it wouldn't have been the mouse that roared.)

—Luci Swindoll
I Married Adventure

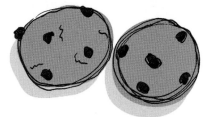

Let's Keep Things in Perspective

◎ Amazing! You just hang something in your closet for a while, and it shrinks two sizes.

◎ There are two kinds of women who will pay big bucks for a makeup mirror that magnifies their faces. The first are young models who need to be sure to cover every eyelash and define their lips. The second are women who, without their glasses, can't even find their faces.

◎ A balanced diet is a cookie in each hand.

◎ There are many women like me who talk about cosmetic surgery, but our philosophy prevails: No guts — live with the ruts.

— Barbara Johnson
Leaking Laffs

I like to think Psalm 16:6 (KJV)
is talking about laugh lines
and good genes
rather than land boundaries:
"The lines are fallen unto me
in pleasant places;
yes, I have a goodly heritage."

Barbara Johnson

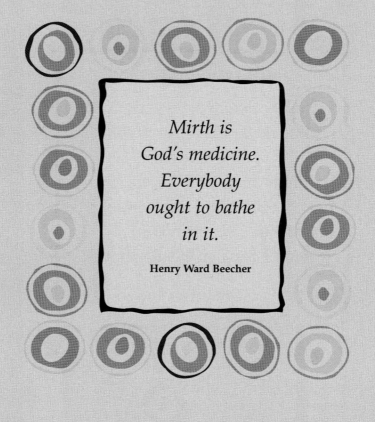

*Mirth is
God's medicine.
Everybody
ought to bathe
in it.*

Henry Ward Beecher

Just for Laughs

I was about five years old when I was standing on my tiptoes to get a drink from the water fountain at church. It was between Sunday school and worship service, so the hallway was filled with folks heading to the sanctuary and others slipping out the side door for their cars. As I drank down the cool water, I could hear two gray haired, been-around-for-years saints of the church whispering to one another as they slipped in line behind me. One patted me gently on the back of the head and said to her friend, "This is one of our preacher's daughters. She's not very p-r-e-t-t-y."

I turned around and in a matter-of-fact way answered, "No. But I'm real s-m-a-r-t!"

—**Chonda Pierce**
Second Row, Piano Side

Still Laughing About It

$\mathcal{I}$ called a Christian publishing company to ask about a bill I'd received by mistake. The man who answered my call said he didn't handle billing questions. Instead, he politely asked me to call a different number. He fumbled around on his desk, apparently looking for his phone list. "Here it is," he said and read off a number.

I called it and was automatically put on hold for a long time, listening to endless repetitions of songs like "Strangers in the Night" and "Who's that Girl?" *Strange music for a Christian organization*, I mused as I waited.

Finally, a woman came on the line. I laid out my question about the bill. "Uh, I think you have the wrong number," she said.

I read the telephone number back to her, asking if I had misdialed.

"That's our number," she answered slowly. "But we don't do Christian publishing. We're a dating service for nudists."

"I've called a *dating* service for *nudists*?" I gasped.

"Yes ma'am. Sunshine Sweethearts."

I could hardly wait to call back the man at the publishing company. Redialing his number, it occurred to me that I had a choice to make: I could indignantly scold him for referring me to a company of dubious moral standing, or I could laugh about the mix-up and invite him to join me.

Do you have any doubt which choice I made? If so, just listen. You'll probably hear us laughing about it still.

—Barbara Johnson
The Great Adventure

No, Not Bungee Jumping!

When was the last time you tried something outside your comfort zone? I'm not thinking of anything as radical as bulging your corneas with bungee jumping. No, I have in mind expanding your sense of yourself in an artistic adventure.

I have a number of friends who have tried their hands at painting. Some chose watercolors, others oils, while still others dabbled with acrylics. Across the board they had wonderful results.

We owe it to ourselves to make room for artistic expression. After all, the creative process puts us in touch with the Creator.

—Patsy Clairmont
The Great Adventure

FABULOUS YOU!

Be yourself ... and love it!

Repeat After Me

I believe in affirmations. An affirmation is a positive statement spoken in first-person singular, present tense, as if it had already happened. Here are some affirmations. Repeat them after me:

"I like myself."

"Things work out well for me."

"I am attractive and charming."

"I enjoy life."

"I am blessed."

"I like people."

"I am successful."

"I love my family."

"I have all the money I need to do whatever I want."

Now stop laughing. If you keep saying it and working toward it, you'll make room in your life for God to make it all come true.

—Thelma Wells
Girl, Have I Got Good News for You

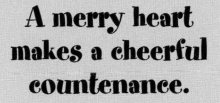

A merry heart makes a cheerful countenance.

Proverbs 15:13

The LORD has done great things for us, and we are glad.

Psalm 126:3

Break Out of Your Little Plastic Mold

*H*ow long has it been since YOU did something outrageous? How long has it been since you ate watermelon and tried to see how far you could spit the seeds? Or gathered big armfuls of lilacs and brought them to friends so their homes would smell like spring? Or marched in a parade or climbed *up* the down escalator? Take a chance. Break out of your little plastic mold and become a DINGY person (not a din-gee but DING-ee) even if people think you are fresh out of the rubber-room situation.

Did you ever watch a child swat madly at specks of dust hanging suspended in a shaft of sunlight?

Children delight at such innocent, simple things—
and so can you. Become a child again. Laugh! It's
like jogging on the inside. Look for ways to enjoy
your day—however small or trivial—even finding a
convenient parking space! Look at a field of flowers
and see FLOWERS, not WEEDS!

—Barbara Johnson
Living Somewhere Between Estrogen and Death

The most interesting
people I know
drink in life
and savor every drop—
the sweet and the sour.
The good and the bad.
The planned
and the unplanned.

Luci Swindoll

The Lens of Possibility

What if everybody in the whole world decided to start looking at life through the lens of possibility? There would be no boring people. There would be no average days. There would be no mediocre activity. There would be no reason for prolonged discouragement—nothing to hold us back from conquering the enemies that steal our joy or disturb our souls. Everything would be possible because our focus would be on the Lord Jesus, who makes all things possible.

—Luci Swindoll
I Married Adventure

God Created You!

$\mathcal{J}$ust imagine how heaven grew silent and God's heart swelled with joy when —"Whaaaaaa!"—you arrived on earth to become, to be, to live! Another baby girl, created by Him was born! God is crazy about you! From the moment of your conception, He hovered over every week of your growth in the womb as you came to resemble more and more the person He designed you to be. He watched intently as you made your way into the world, screaming, writing, and adjusting to earth's air. His complex little girl had been launched on her journey, which already was recorded in His book.

He knew your beginning.

He knew the family that would shape you.

And yes, He even knew the struggles you would have along the way.

He knew them then and He knows them now. You can say without doubt, "How precious are your thoughts about me, O God."

—Jan Silvious
Big Girls Don't Whine

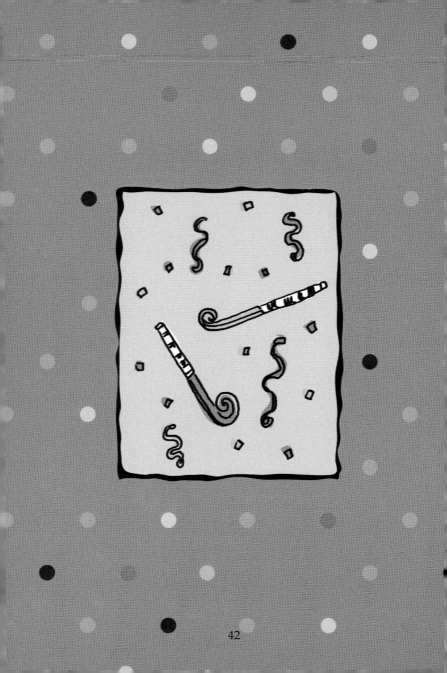

Encouragement— Spiritual Confetti!

I love throwing things up in the air. At weddings, or on New Year's Eve, everybody wants something in their hands to throw. It's a way of lavishing our love on people. Confetti is a tangible expression of intangible emotions. No celebration is complete without it.

Taking the time to gather little pieces of love, grace, strength, and hope is worth it when you shower your friendships with them. Spiritual confetti! It is the ultimate encouragement. . . .

Encouragement is to a friendship what confetti is to a party. It's light, refreshing, and fun, and you always end up finding little pieces of it stuck on you later.

—**Nicole Johnson**
Fresh-Brewed Life

43

Get Messy!

*T*oo often we play it safe in life because we're afraid of making mistakes. But God is a God of color, of light. He is creative and spectacular in every way. He doesn't hold back in His self-expression!

The great Master Painter allows you and me to take up our little brushes and paint our lives in a multitude of colors — some that clash, some that take others by surprise or provoke disapproval. In all of this He looks down on us in love, He smiles, He celebrates our uniqueness.

So take risks with your kids. Do crazy things. Surprise your husband. Have dinner all set up in the yard with candles and music. Dress in a whole new style. Change your hairstyle or color. Paint a wall — every wall! If you've seen the television show *The Magic School Bus*, you'll remember Miss Frizzel's motto: "Take chances, get messy, make mistakes." Amen, Miss Frizzel!

— Sheila Walsh
The Great Adventure

Just because it hasn't
been done before
doesn't mean you
shouldn't try it.

Howard Shultz

*Pleasure lies
in the heart,
not in the
happenstance.*

The Art of Savoring Life

To experience happiness we must train ourselves to live in this moment, to savor it for what it is, not running ahead in anticipation of some future date nor lagging behind in the paralysis of the past. With wholeness and sensitivity we must live in the here and now. "But what if I don't like the here and now?" you ask. "What if my present moment is one of disappointment or impairment or heartache? How then do I savor that moment?" Good questions.

The answers reside in the first and most profound principle for the art of savoring life: *Pleasure lies in the heart, not in the happenstance.*

— Luci Swindoll
You Bring the Confetti

Keep Dancing

The ballet days of my youth continue to hold fond memories for me. On Saturday mornings, when I was ten years old, I would bound out of bed, dress, grab my ballet slippers, and walk a half-mile to my ballet class. Trust me, it takes a lot for me to bound in the morning, but dance motivated me.

Truth be told, I still have my ballet slippers. Does it seem silly that I've saved them all these years? I think I believed that one day I would use them again. But now my years have stockpiled into a stack higher than I'm tall. Besides, at this point in my journey, I couldn't fit one of those tiny slippers on my bunion much less my puffy feet. Yet when I glance into the guest bedroom and see those sweet slippers hanging on the wall, I have two responses. First, I have a moment of reverie, and then I'm reminded to keep dancing. Oh, not a pirouette (I'm dizzy enough) or even a grand *jeté* (midair leap—ouch), but to move through my remaining days with a toe-tapping melody of joy.

—Patsy Clairmont
The Shoe Box

Apple Muffins

$\mathcal{O}$ne of my favorite foods on earth is fresh, hot, homemade apple muffins. I make them occasionally when I have time and enjoy one with a fresh-brewed pot of coffee. I take the muffin, the coffee, and the newspaper, and sit on my patio (sometimes with the neighborhood cats) relishing the beginning of a new day. All my senses are pleased. Complete satisfaction.

—Luci Swindoll
I Married Adventure

Apple Muffins

1 3/4 cups flour

2 tsp. baking powder

1 teaspoon cinnamon

1/2 teaspoon nutmeg

pinch of salt

1 egg

1/2 cup brown sugar

1 cup applesauce

1 apple, peeled, seeded, and finely chopped

1/3 cup corn oil

Preheat oven to 350 degrees. Grease a 12-cup muffin pan. Sift the dry ingredients into a large bowl. In another bowl, mix the egg, sugar, applesauce, apple, and oil. Combine the wet ingredients with the dry ingredients. Divide the batter between the 12 muffin cups. Bake for 20-25 minutes. Enjoy!

Create for Thyself a Sundae

I can't count the number of times recently that women who were once real go-getters— intelligent, creative, and energetic—have said to me that they are just tired of life. They are bored with the humdrum of their daily routines and relationships. They see no way out.

I have two words for that kind of thinking. As the kids in my neighborhood would say, "Chill out." You sound like you're overburdened, brain-dead, and on life-support in your mind.

Draw yourself a hot bubble bath tonight and splash around for a while. Thoroughly enjoy the moment. Then, with childlike anticipation, ask your heavenly Father, "Now what?" The answer might be, "Get yourself to bed, woman! You're whipped!" Or it might be something totally outside your routine, like "Go ye into the kitchen at midnight and create for thyself a sundae with every kind of dollop and sprinkle ye can find."

You never know what you might be missing if you grow up too much and stop asking, "Now what?"

— Thelma Wells
The Great Adventure

Fully Alive

$\mathcal{M}$y mom has an unusual style of piano playing. She uses only the black keys. One day as a kid I asked her, "Why do you play only on the black notes?" I had started piano lessons and knew that this was not the correct way.

"I taught myself to play when I was a child," she said. "I play by ear, and this is the only way I can do it."

It was a familiar sound to me and I loved it, but I realized sometime later that our old piano was capable of so much more. My sister, Frances, dated a boy from school, and one night when he was over for dinner he sat down at the piano and played. When Ian used all the keys, the piano sounded like a different instrument.

We were made for the joy and laughter of the major keys, and also for the pain and tears of the minor. Part of being fully alive to God is being willing to embrace *all* that He puts in our path.

— **Sheila Walsh**
Gifts for Your Soul

My Bunny Slippers

$\mathcal{A}$ friend sent me a pair of bunny slippers, and every now and then I put them on, especially when I'm tempted to start thinking I'm important or "nearly famous." There's something about bunny slippers that keeps my perspective where it belongs, but in addition to that, my bunny slippers remind me that whatever happens doesn't have to get me down. I can still be a little silly and laugh and enjoy life. Pain dissolves, frustrations vanish, and burdens roll away when I have on my bunny slippers.

—**Barbara Johnson**
Mama, Get the Hammer!

So Much Fun!

Sometimes I have the feeling I'm the quintessential pioneer gal who just happens to be living in the twenty-first century. Ask my friends. They'll tell you. There's little about me that's stylish, I don't like many new or fancy things, and I've been known to give gifts made from trash. Put that all together and, honey, it spells Country Woman.

In fact, I sort of wish I owned a truck—maybe an old '56 Ford pickup. That'd be great. I could drive it down to the Farmer's Market for fresh produce and cut flowers, or I could haul shingles if I decided to put a new roof on the house. Pickups come in handy.

Life has so much fun in it. Little things can thrill us to pieces when we make curiosity our guide. Sometimes we miss the joy and excitement of living because we're so busy looking for something expensive or out of the ordinary to give us a rush. It doesn't occur to us that everyday experiences have built-in challenge and thrills.

Why not experiment a little with a meal or a project? Try looking at it in a new and different way. The Lord gives us everything we need to cook up adventure. We don't have to leave home to find it. We don't need money or time. We simply need to ask the Lord, "What do I look for?" —and He'll show us the fun right in front of us.

—Luci Swindoll
The Great Adventure

Fresh Ideas

In the Academy Award-nominated movie *Il Postino (The Postman)*, a common postman seeks to woo the lady of his dreams and beseeches Pablo Neruda, a world-famous poet, to help him. Neruda advises him, "Speak in similes, master the metaphor." The postman struggles with the concept, until Neruda asks him to explain how this woman makes him feel. He begins, "Her eyes are the color of this sea before us, changing moods and greens and blues." "That's it!" cries Neruda. "You've done it! You've just created a metaphor!" The postman exultantly writes it down, hands it to the heretofore uninterested lady, and ultimately wins her heart by comparing her to nature . . . using similes and metaphors.

There are few gifts more valuable to a great communicator than being able to link seemingly dissimilar objects, creating fresh ideas and color-filled associations. Writers, poets, artists, sculptors, and musicians are essentially engaged in the business of mastering metaphors, communicating thoughts and ideas that teach us how to look again.

—Laurie Beth Jones
Jesus in Blue Jeans

Squiggles of Enjoyment

There are a thousand tiny things from which one can weave a bright necklace of little pleasures for one's life.

Hermann Hesse

What are the tiny joys from which you can "weave a bright necklace of pleasure?" For me there is always that which appeals to my senses. There are certain smells that invariably put me into orbit: fresh cut grass, lilacs in the spring, roses, the earth after a rain, mountain air, fresh baked bread. . . . Then there is the joy of seeing the glory of nature — the sky, a tree, the ocean, a flower, the Colorado Rocky Mountains. There is the joy of feeling the smoothness of pebbles washed clean by the repeated pounding of the surf.

One of my favorite sensations comes from drinking tea from a china cup I inherited from my grandmother's collection. It is French Haviland china and more than one hundred years old. It is so thin, so exquisitely delicate, that if I hold it to the light, it is possible to see shadows of the images beyond it. . . .

I'm sure you could add many more to this short list of little pleasures that guarantee an occasional squiggle of enjoyment.

—Marilyn Meberg
Choosing the Amusing

A list of my favorite squiggles
of enjoyment:

_____

_____

_____

_____

_____

_____

_____

_____

_____

_____

FAMILY

It's about
loving,
sharing,
and
connecting.

Coffee and Cake

$\mathcal{M}$y mother's mother, Audrey, introduced me to coffee. She would make me coffee-milk in the mornings before anyone else got up. I must have been four or five, and, holding my current favorite stuffed companion and still sucking my thumb, I would pad sleepy-eyed into the kitchen where the kettle was boiling. The only light in the room was the one on the stove, and my grandmother would be sitting on a stool next to the counter, sipping coffee. She would get up and begin to fix my coffee-milk. Sweet and warm beyond compare. Sharing a cup became our secret ritual. I thought it was my reward for waking up early. She would pull me up a chair, and we would talk for a bit. I felt so grown up. . . .

My father's brother and sisters needed nothing more than a coffeepot for celebration. Okay, maybe one of Grandma's caramel cakes helped a bit. They would sit for hours with coffee and one another. I would take it all in, learning what "coffee" meant to them: love, sharing, and connection.

—Nicole Johnson
Fresh-Brewed Life

This Was No Dream

$\mathcal{T}$ he lightning bolt of a lifetime struck . . . when we we returned from our honeymoon to the old place we were renting from my father-in-law for free. . . . There was no dishwasher, no garbage disposal, and no money. The only thing that house had plenty of was deer heads. They were everywhere. And they seemed to stare at me as if I had sold out. They did lead to the purchase of a secondhand dryer, however. Keith bought one the day after he came in with a friend and found our underwear dangling from their horns. I think that may have been the first time anyone had ever called me "sacrilegious."

My groom . . . worked long hours out in the heat and worked with people who had no teeth. Then he'd walk in the door, say he was starving, and look at me as if he expected me to do something about it. Think as I may, I cannot for the life of me remember a kitchen in the Barbie Dream House. Then it hit me. I wasn't Barbie. He wasn't Ken. This was no dream. And I wanted my mother. . . .

We've suffered our share of bumps and bruises over the years since we drove off in our Barbie dream car and had a head-on collision with reality. We've grown up a little and grown together a lot. We had entered marriage each carrying a deluxe, five-piece set of emotional baggage, certain our own was heavier than the other's. We had expectations that exceeded the realm of possibility. I have finally forgiven Keith for not being Ken. I've almost forgiven myself for not being Barbie. And by the grace of God, we've made it in spite of ourselves.

— Beth Moore
Things Pondered

On the pleasant days of
marriage, gaze across
at your groom and conclude he
is worth it. On the difficult
days of marriage gaze up
at your Groom and conclude
He's worth it.

Beth Moore

Wring Out All the Joy

People often ask me, "Why are you so happy all the time?" Well, I'm happy because when I wake up in the morning, I don't read my name in the obituaries! I'm alive, and I've been given the gift of one more day. Life is precious, and every day is a new opportunity; I want to wring all the joy out of it that I possibly can.

Now, admittedly, someone with this demeanor often stands out in the crowd (especially if the crowd is feeling cranky that day). I once overheard a woman ask my daughter Vikki, "Is your mother happy like this all the time?" She meant did I laugh and seem to enjoy life all the time.

If Vikki were one to roll her eyes, she might have rolled them then. "Yes," she replied with a sigh. "She makes me tired. I can't even have a bad day around her. You know, some days I just want to feel sorry for myself, but you can't be around Mama and be sad for long."

Well, I took that as a compliment! I'm glad she can't have a bad day around me. Why would anybody want to have a bad day anyway?

— Thelma Wells
The Buzz

A Fully Functioning Woman

My friend Edna used to make me smile with her replies when people asked her when she was going to get married. One time she said, in response to the when-will-you-get-married question, "Oh, he died in the war." The person gulped and mumbled, "Oh, I'm sorry. I didn't know." Then Edna said, "He must have, he never showed up!" It was all I could do to keep from giggling out loud. Edna has a great perspective on life. She has lived as a fully functioning woman with great joy even though she is single. (Or maybe I should say *because* she is single.)

The principle truth that every woman has to grab hold of, whether single, married, divorced, or widowed is this: You are valuable just because you are you. God has plans for you just because you are you. You came into the world alone, you will leave alone, and you will give an account—alone. The relationships you develop along life's journey may be highly significant and part of God's plan, but they do not define you. You are precious by yourself and God is crazy about you.

—**Jan Silvious**
Big Girls Don't Whine

Love Is Easy to Spot

The year the new VW Bug® came out, my mother-in-law bought one. Aren't they just the cutest little cars? Hers is black, and she keeps the little bud vase in the dashboard stocked with a spray of pink roses—her signature flower. She named the car Sophia. My children all know that Grandma drives a black bug, and even a one-year-old can distinguish a VW Bug® from the other cars in traffic.

Everywhere we go, from the freeways to back ways, the kids pick them out—red ones, yellow ones, blue ones, and lime green ones. And invariably they will sing out "I see a Bug! Is it Grandma?"

Jesus told us that, because of our love for others, we would be easy to pick out in this world—just like a VW Bug® is easy to spot on the freeway. We'll stand out because we're different. "By this all will know that you are My disciples, if you have love one for another "(John 13:35). Do you stand out in the crowd?

—Christa Kinde
Encouraging One Another

Savor life as you would
a latté—
one drop at a time.

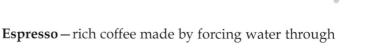

Espresso—rich coffee made by forcing water through finely ground, dark roasted coffee beans

Latté—espresso with steamed milk

Café au lait—equal parts espresso and steamed milk

Mocha—latté with a little bit of chocolate

Café breve—espresso with steamed Half and Half

Espresso com panna—a serving of espresso topped with a dollop of sweetened whipped cream

Iced espresso—a double espresso poured over crushed ice

Iced cappuccino—single or double serving of espresso poured over crushed ice and topped with an ounce or two of cold milk

Back to Grilled Cheese

There came a brief time when the realization that "We are poor" hit us all. Mother couldn't find a job. Dad had just accepted a call to a small church in Orangeburg, South Carolina. Mike had gone to a college 500 miles away, and Charlotta was soon to follow. I can remember hearing Mom and Dad argue about the possibility of getting food stamps. I don't think it was as much a matter of pride as it was that Mom still didn't consider us desperate enough. She would say, "But what if someone else needs them more?"

As I sat at the dinner table eating for the fifth time that week a sandwich made with government cheese and grilled with government butter, I looked at her and said, "Mom, who could need 'em worse than us?"

So one afternoon Mom and I stood in the food stamp line for more than three hours. Of course, after we got them, the whole family wanted in on the selection process at the grocery store. Grocery shopping had never been so exciting. Everyone was thrilled to pick out the food, but as soon as we approached the checkout counter, they all scrambled to the car—except for Mom and me. When Mother handed the girl at the Piggy Wiggly our little booklet, I grinned at Mother and said in my most Southern-belle, Scarlet O'Hara voice, "I'll tell the driver to bring the limo around, Mother, and pick us up at the door. I know how you hate to wait in this summer heat."

When the food stamps ran out, we went back to grilled cheese until things began to pick up at the church again.

—Chonda Pierce
Second Row, Piano Side

What Did the Doctor Say?

A woman accompanied her husband to the doctor's office for a checkup. Afterward, the physician asked to speak to the wife alone. He told her, "Your husband has a serious problem. Unless you do the following things for him, he will surely die. First, you need to make sure he gets a good, healthy breakfast every morning. Then, have him come home for lunch every day and feed him a well-balanced meal. Make sure you feed him a good, hot, nutritious dinner every night. Also, you must keep the house spotless and clean so he won't be exposed to any unnecessary germs. And finally, don't burden him with household chores."

As they settled into the car for the ride home, the husband asked his wife, "Well, what did the doctor tell you about my condition?"

The wife replied, "He said you're going to die."

As a wife who gave up cooking long ago and who considers dust a decorative item, I laugh every time I hear that story. Oddly enough, my husband doesn't think it's funny.

— Barbara Johnson
The Great Adventure

The Promise of the Morning

I have never been a morning person, so it was a rude awakening when baby Christian came along. I remember saying to my mom that I would need to buy a new alarm clock so I could wake up and feed the baby. She laughed. I didn't know then that babies come fully equipped with their own, not-to-be-ignored alarm.

As Christians, we all are morning people. We live now, as C. S. Lewis said, in the shadowlands, and we wait for morning.

Whatever you're going through at the moment, remember this is not the end of your story. We are morning people, called to live by faith and not by sight, to lift our hearts to God in the darkness because we have the promise of the morning.

—**Sheila Walsh**
We Brake for Joy

Faith

He will yet fill your mouth
with laughing.

Job 8:21

Love Is the Laughter of God

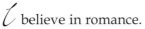

I believe in romance.

Romance. Not fairy tales. There's nothing like love to awaken a soul to the realization that if fairies *did* exist, they told a serious *tale.* Cinderella soon discovered that Prince Charming could smell a lot like his horse. Snow White sometimes thought she'd rather go home to the seven dwarves. Rapunzel found herself wishing she'd had a crew cut. The princess who kissed the frog recognized some of the same warts on her prince. Love tends to be blind only in the beginning. How else would we take the risk? Oh, but love is worth the risk when our hearts belong to God.

Human love is always imperfect love, but God has sentimentally chosen to whisper hints of the perfect through its imperfections. Through the flawed, He kindles faith for the flawless, awakening the mortal heart to a brush with the immortal. Such love suggests that there is still stuff of heaven falling to earth. For true love is by its nature selfless, sacrificial . . . and there is nothing in the heart of man so divine. It is a gift of God.

—Beth Moore
Feathers from My Nest

Sarah Laughed

Laughter must be pretty important to God or He wouldn't have spent so much time talking about it. Depending on which version of the Bible you study, the word *laughter* appears about forty times. One of my favorite laughter verses is part of the Old Testament story of Abraham and his wife, Sarah, who gave birth when Abraham was one hundred years old and Sarah herself was well past her child-bearing years. When their son Isaac was miraculously born, Sarah said, "God has brought me laughter, and everyone who hears about this will laugh with me" (Gen. 21:6, NIV).

Frankly, I don't know too many women today who would think it was funny to have a new baby in their old age. Having a hundred-year-old husband to care for would be hard enough, let alone an infant too! But God had promised Abraham and Sarah a family, and when that promise was fulfilled, Sarah laughed with delight. I'm guessing that joy-filled attitude worked like a daily dose of vitamins, keeping Sarah going so she could be a good mother to her son and a loving wife to her husband. She knew the wisdom expressed in Proverbs 17:22 (NKJV): "A merry heart does good, like medicine."

—Thelma Wells
The Buzz

A Cheerful Heart

*G*od means for us to experience joy. It is not His intent that we suffer from ulcers, migraine headaches, and other stress-related illnesses. Review with me these scriptures that remind us what God says about joy.

> *"A cheerful heart has a continual feast."*
> (Proverbs 15:15)

> *"A joyful heart makes a cheerful face."*
> (Proverbs 15:13)

God has given to each of us an incomparable medicine bag—in it is the divinely created ability to laugh at ourselves, at our circumstances, at humor produced by others, and to take a less threatened view of everything around us. To utilize the contents of that bag is to experience healing for our minds, our souls, and our bodies.

—Marilyn Meberg
Choosing the Amusing

*When you have nothing
to laugh about, laugh anyway.
Soon you'll feel
the healing power
of joy and laughter
bringing new energy and life
to your weary,
frustrating day.*

Thelma Wells

The Essence of Joy

The psalmist says, "Delight yourself in the LORD and He will give you the desires of your heart" (Psalm 37:4). I believe this works two ways. We delight, or find joy, in the Lord, and He gives us our heart's desires. He puts His desires in our hearts and then fulfills them. . . .

Let's get practical. Perhaps you have an idea of something you would like to do, but you're scared. You've never done anything like it before. Maybe the idea just won't go away. But it's outside your comfort zone, and you don't feel adequate for the task. Start to pray, "Lord, if this desire is from you, will you bring it to pass? Help me know where to start."

And then start. This is the faith part. Work hard. Do what makes sense to you. And then do the next thing. . . . This is exactly how I started to write thirteen years ago. Someone challenged me to write a book, and I was scared to death. But God gave me the desire, He answered when I prayed, and it was a delight.

What has He given you the desire to do? You can do it.

— **Luci Swindoll**
We Brake for Joy

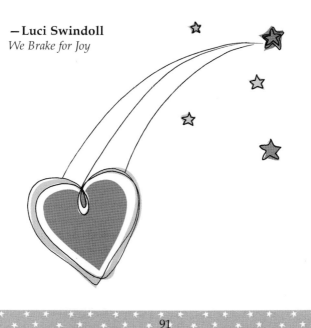

Have a Good Day!

One day I was getting a cup of coffee and a bagel in Colorado Springs. I commented to the waitress that I hoped she had a good rest of the day. "How can it be good when I'm working?" she asked. I told her, "Don't postpone your life until you get off. Just think about at work what you would think about if you weren't working." She smiled and then laughed. "I guess I could do that." Sure she could, and so can I. The quality of my day is determined by one thing: my attitude toward it.

—Nicole Johnson
Fresh-Brewed Life

You Can Praise or Pout

$\mathcal{W}$hen the stress piles up and you are disappointed with how things are going, you have a choice. You can praise or you can pout. That's what it amounts to. You can make the conscious decision to be grateful to this God who is in control, or you can pout because things haven't gone your way.

There are plenty of situations that can bring your spirits down. When things aren't going well, we can blame God for what is wrong and retreat to our personal arena of pouting and self-pity, or we can make a choice to praise Him for who He is. When we praise God in the midst of negative circumstances, we are choosing to trust that He is loving and good. Such praise is sweet to Him because it honors Him for who He is—God—and not because He has given us what we want in life.

—Jan Silvous
Look at It This Way

Tell God the Truth

It's not my place to judge anyone's prayers, but I think God would be honored with a bit more honesty. He made our hearts, and He knows what's in them.

I love the story of the dinner party where the father asked his six-year-old daughter to bless the meal in front of their evening guests.

"But I don't know what to say," the little girl replied.

He coaxed her some more. "Just say what you've heard Mommy say."

"Dear Lord," she began, "why did I invite all these people to dinner?"

Prayer is the safest place to tell the truth.

—Nicole Johnson
Fresh-Brewed Life

Steady, Measured Steps

One day, my husband took up racquetball. Knowing I needed the exercise, I also ventured into the little box that was the court. It seemed a trifle small for the two of us, but it was fun. Having played tennis years ago, in the days of my youth, I managed quite well. However, being thoroughly out of shape, I found myself running furiously in every direction for about twenty minutes and then suddenly collapsing in a whimpering heap in a corner of the court.

My experience reminded me of the Christian life. The journey of faith is not a step or leap. It is supposed to be a steady, daily walking along the path of God for your life. The idea is to plod with God, rather than to race through space! Sitting exhausted in a hotel chair, American pastor Vance Havner was asked by a lady in his group if he was enjoying his tour of Jerusalem. He replied, "Madam, I am pooped. Today I ran where Jesus walked!" Those of us who have been on such tours understand how he felt. But you know, we are not intended to "run where Jesus walked." We are to walk with steady, measured tread in the steps of the Master.

—**Jill Briscoe**
Here Am I Lord

When talking about yourself, speak words of hope, health, encouragement, life, and purpose. They are God's truth for you.

Stormie Omartian

God Can!

I've had my inadequate moments. Growing up,
I felt awkward and ugly in comparison to my
beautiful sister. I knew the boys wanted to get to
know me only so they could get to know her!
We feel inadequate a thousand times a day, about
a thousand different things.

The release comes when first you realize you are
indeed hopelessly inadequate, and then you realize
for this you have God! You can't; He can! You are
inadequate; He isn't!

—Jill Briscoe
Here Am I, Lord

"Mirror Mirror"

Any Age Is Beautiful!

To grow older joyfully means to accept what is. This implies we determine to live with the reality that says we are truly the age we are, to date. Any age is beautiful because life itself is a beautiful thing. As Mark Twain once said, "Age is mostly a matter of mind. If you don't mind, it doesn't matter." Where we get into trouble is the attempt to be something

we are not, whether that's in our age or in our person. Such inner deception can also lead to self-defeat and depression.

We are the most appealing to others, and the happiest within when we are completely ourselves. But it is a constant struggle because, as Scripture teaches, the world is always trying to press us into its mold. The mold of the world is the mold of the synthetic . . . the artificial . . . the celluloid—the "Plastic Person." The world cries, "You've got to be thin and you've got to be rich. You've got to be great." But Scripture says, "You don't have to be any of those things. You simply have to be yourself—at any age as God made you, available to Him so that He can work in and through you to bring about His kingdom and His glory."

—**Luci Swindoll**
You Bring the Confetti

Partnering with God

Computers are utterly inexplicable to me. Not only that, but they also have an attitude. At least mine does! For instance, something as simple as closing out a program and shutting down the computer sends the little demonic person who scowlingly sits inside the machine day and night into parental mode. A question flashes on the screen: "Are you sure you want to shut down your machine?" Until the question was asked, I was quite certain I wanted to shut it down, but with those bold words glaring at me, I hesitate. Maybe I was wrong. Does the little machine person know something I don't? Will something irreparable happen if it shuts down?

Not wanting to appear uncertain, I click yes. But my self-confidence is undermined, and I wait nervously for the whole thing to explode all over my lap.

Life is filled with annoying little cheer depleters. I have often pondered how many of these little imperfections to bring to God's attention and how many to simply pass off. Will my cheer increase if I talk to God about the things that don't work? Is it reasonable as I walk into the office supply store to ask God to help me find the fax machine paper that doesn't curl up like a scroll the minute it exits my machine?

I am gradually beginning to understand that the notion of bringing God into everything has nothing to do with trivializing Him; it has to do with the privilege of partnering with Him.

— Marilyn Meberg
I'd Rather Be Laughing

Laugh-out-loud lines from Barbara Johnson:

❋ Frogs have it easy; they can eat what bugs them.

❋ Patience is the ability to count down before blasting off.

❋ Sometimes it's hard to soar with the eagles because of all the turkeys in your life.

Laughter is like changing a baby's diaper; it doesn't permanently solve any problems but it does make things more acceptable for a while.

Smile! It kills time between disasters.

Life is like an ice cream cone: Just when you think you've got it licked, it drips all over you!

There is hope for any woman who can look in a mirror and laugh at what she sees.

If at first you don't succeed, see if the loser gets anything.

Feeling Underestimated?

The media escort who accompanied me on the Los Angeles stop of my most recent book tour was a woman about five-feet two inches tall. A petite blond with movie star charisma, she disclosed during our conversation that after she had been mugged and later car-jacked in Los Angeles, she had become a black belt kick boxer. Now, when she and her husband encounter rough situations, her six-foot one-inch husband whispers, "Go ahead, honey, get 'em. I'll hold your purse." She says she actually enjoys the feeling of being underestimated.

Unless you are dealing with people who daily recognize and acknowledge the miracle-working power of God, chances are very good you are being underestimated, and more significantly, chances are you are underestimating yourself.

When we have access, through prayer and meditation, to all the gifts and knowledge of God, we can be relatively confident that whoever is challenging us is underestimating us. Our responsibility in difficult situations is to harness the power of God in us, and the power of God everywhere.

—Laurie Beth Jones
Jesus in Blue Jeans

Quiet Companionship

Recently I saw a silly cartoon that depicted a stout little bearded fellow wearing a biblical-era robe and smiling in the midst of two giraffes, two dogs, two elephants, two snakes, and several other pairs of creatures. The little man and his animals were gathered around a big sign near a gate that said, "Noah's Park." The voice coming down from above said something like, "Okay, now, let's try it again. And this time listen carefully!" . . .

There are times when God's will isn't obvious to us. Do we stay in this job or accept another offer? . . . Should we enroll our kids in public school or private? How do we decide which choice God wants us to make?

The Bible says Noah "walked with God" (Genesis 6:9). It doesn't say he *talked* with God. Instead the image implies quiet companionship. . . . Noah spent time with the Father, and during their time together God spoke to him. And as outrageous as God's instructions may have seemed at the time, Noah set about building an ark. He stepped out with courage to do what he perceived as God's will.

— Barbara Johnson
Outrageous Joy

We are not troubled
by the things
that happen to us,
but by our opinion
of the things
that happen to us.

Anonymous

Holes in My Earlobes

I sat pinched and tense on a padded stool in a jewelry store in the mall. In the mirror I watched the woman standing behind me. She held a small, shiny gun pointed to the ceiling, and she grinned. "You might feel a little sting." She grabbed hold of one of my earlobes and brought her gun down to meet it. I closed my eyes, and my momma's words rang loud in my ears: "If the Lord had meant for you to have holes in your earlobes, He would have put them there!"

I grew up with two sisters, and we heard that a lot. But I was eighteen and in college now; I had moved out of our house and into the dorm. So I had marched into the jewelry store with an air of defiance, and I had told the woman behind the counter, "Pierce my ears. I am a woman . . . *and my momma's not here!*"

All it took was two quick shots. Ouch! Ouch! I had holes in both earlobes.

When I walked out the door, I had taken only a couple of steps, with the tiny starter set shining in my sore earlobes, when two nuns dressed in black and white walked by. I just knew it was a sign from God! I took those earrings out right there and never put them in again.

Until I work up the nerve to try again, clip-ons work fine for me. Besides, should Gabriel blow his trumpet while I'm sporting a pair of earbobs, I can slip those things right off and I'll be ready to go! Some of these young people today are going to have a hard time. They had better hope it's a *long* song — long enough to pull out everything from their ears, noses, cheeks, tongues, and belly buttons!

—Chonda Pierce
I Can See Myself in His Eyeballs

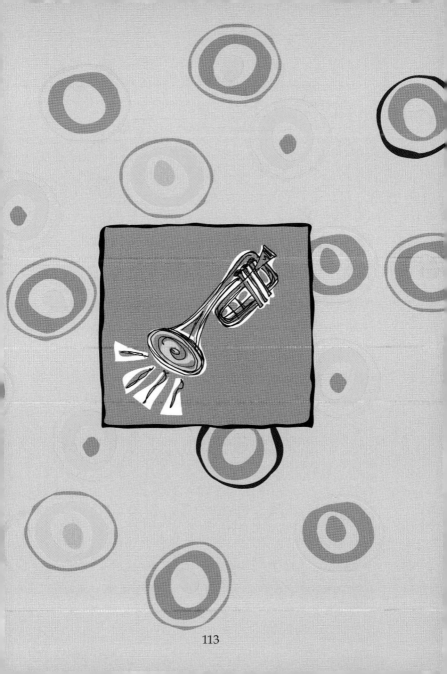

A Heart Full of Joy

*J*oy is like a bouquet of balloons from Jesus meant to hearten us. Not the circus kind that float willy-nilly, but the hot air kind that have a predetermined direction. I believe we enter into our joy as we determine to tilt our hearts upward, for an upward tilt allows us to receive all He has to offer. . . .

The outrageous women I work with are some of the most joyful women I have ever known. . . . At our conferences Thelma sings, "I've got the joy, joy, joy, joy down in my heart." If you sang this song in Sunday school, you know that the question is then sung out, "Where?" and the response is an affirmative "Down in my heart!" Why? To remind us that this is an inside job between the Lord and us. He gives us joy, and then we choose to respond out of it. Which takes us back to the tilt of our heart. The more receptive we are to the Lord, the more likely we are to have the joy, joy, joy, joy way down in the depths of our hearts.

—Patsy Clairmont
Outrageous Joy

Acknowledgements

Grateful acknowledgment is made to the following publishers for permission to reprint this copyrighted material.

Jill Briscoe ©, *Here am I, Lord, . . . Send Somebody Else* (Nashville: W Publishing Group, 2004)
Patsy Clairmont ©, *The Shoe Box* (Nashville: W. Publishing Group, 2003)
Barbara Johnson ©, *Mamma, Get the Hammer!* (Nashville: W. Publishing Group, 1994).
Barbara Johnson ©, *Living Somewhere Between Estrogen and Death* (Nashville: W. Publishing Group, 1997).
Barbara Johnson ©, *He's Gonna Toot, and I'm Gonna Scoot* (Nashville: W. Publishing Group, 1999).
Barbara Johnson ©, *Leaking Laffs Between Pampers and Depends* (Nashville: W. Publishing Group, 2000).
Nicole Johnson ©, *Fresh-Brewed Life* (Nashville: W. Publishing Group, 1999)
Carol Kent ©, *Detours, Tow Trucks, and Angels in Disguise* (Colorado Springs: NavPress, 1996).
Laurie Beth Jones ©, *Jesus in Blue Jeans* (New York: Hyperion, 1997).
Marilyn Meberg ©, *I'd Rather Be Laughing* (Nashville: W. Publishing Group, 1998)
Marilyn Meberg ©, *Choosing the Amusing* (Nashville: W. Publishing Group, 1999)
Beth Moore ©, *Things Pondered: From the Heart of a Lesser Woman* (Nashville: Broadman & Holman, Publishers, 1997).
Beth Moore ©, *Feathers from My Nest: A Mother's Reflections* (Nashville: Broadman & Holman, Publishers, 2001).
Chonda Pierce©, *I Can See Myself in His Eyeballs* (Grand Rapids: Zondervan, 2001).
Chonda Pierce, *Second Row, Piano Side* (Kansas City:

Beacon Hill Press©, 1996).

Jan Silvious ©, *Big Girls Don't Whine* (Nashville: W. Publishing Group, 2003)

Jan Silvious ©, *Look at It This Way: Straightforward Wisdom to Put Life in Perspective* (Colorado Springs: WaterBrook Press, 2003)

Luci Swindoll ©, *You Bring the Confetti* (Nashville: W. Publishing Group, 1986)

Luci Swindoll ©, *I Married Adventure* (Nashville: W. Publishing Group, 2002)

Luci Swindoll ©, *Notes to a Working Woman: Finding Balance, Passion, and Fulfillment in Your Life* (Nashville: W. Publishing Group, 1997)

Sheila Walsh ©, *Gifts for Your Soul* (Grand Rapids: Zondervan Publishing House, 1997)

Thelma Wells ©, *Girl, Have I Got Good News for You* (Nashville: W Publishing Group, 2000)

Thelma Wells ©, *The Buzz: Seven Power-Packed Scriptures to Energize Your Life* (Nashville: W Publishing Group, 2004)

Women of Faith ©, *We Brake for Joy: 90 Devotions to Add Laughter, Fun, and Faith to Your Life* (Grand Rapids: Zondervan Publishing House, 1998)

Women of Faith ©, *Outrageous Joy: The Life-Changing, Soul-Shaking Truth About God* (Grand Rapids: Zondervan Publishing House, 1999)

Women of Faith ©, *The Great Adventure: A Devotional Journey of the Heart, Soul, and Mind* (Nashville: W. Publishing Group, 2002).

Women of Faith ©, *Women of Faith Study Guide Series*, Christa Kinde, Ed. *Encouraging One Another* (Nashville: Thomas Nelson, Inc., 2004).

Women of Faith ©, *Laughter Is the Spice of Life* (Nashville: W. Publishing Group, 2004).